christmas treats

christmas treats

hamlyn

NOTES

Medium eggs have been used throughout.

A few recipes include nuts or nut derivatives. It is advisable for those with known allergic reactions to nuts and nut derivatives and those who may be potentially vulnerable to these allergies, such as pregnant and nursing mothers, invalids, the elderly, babies and children, to avoid dishes made with nuts and nut oils. It is also prudent to check the labels of prepared ingredients for the possible inclusion of nut derivatives. Vulnerable people should avoid dishes containing raw or lightly cooked eggs.

Ovens should be preheated to the specified temperature. If using a convection oven, follow the manufacturer's instructions for adjusting the time and temperature.

An Hachette Livre UK Company
www.hachettelivre.co.uk
First published in Great Britain in 2004 by Hamlyn,
a division of Octopus Publishing Group Ltd
2–4 Heron Quays, London E14 4JP
www.octopusbooks.co.uk
Copyright © Octopus Publishing Group Ltd 2004

ISBN 978-0-600-61330-5

A CIP catalogue record for this book is available from the British Library

Printed and bound in China

10 9 8 7 6 5 4

contents

Introduction

Christmas is a time for friends and family, for celebrating in relaxed surroundings with those close to you. This enjoyable time of year is marked by rituals and traditions wherever you are in the world, and this usually includes feasting.

This is the time of year when many people like to treat themselves and their loved ones with home-baked treats, such as biscuits, cakes and sweets. People who rarely bake at other times of the year are often tempted to do so at Christmas to keep the traditions alive. Christmas baking is very satisfying, and homemade cakes and pastries are universally popular, whether eaten at home or given as a delicious gift.

Christmas ingredients
Wherever they originate, traditional Christmas sweets are often made using the same ingredients.
• **Nuts**, such as Brazils, hazelnuts and almonds, are used in cakes, pastries and biscuits.
• **Cranberries** are often served in a savoury sauce along with the Christmas turkey, but they can also make a wonderful ingredient in sweet recipes such as muffins.
• **Dried fruits**, such as raisins, candied peel and dates, are used to make many festive foods, such as Christmas cake, traditional Christmas pudding and mince pies.
• **Marzipan** (almond paste) is used for decoration or to make a sumptuous filling for cakes.
• **Spices** are very popular and transform Christmas sweet treats with their exotic flavours. Cinnamon, nutmeg, ginger and cloves add aroma and spice to many different dishes.

Traditional foods

Most countries that celebrate Christmas have their own Christmas cake. In Britain and the United States, it is a rich fruit cake, sometimes covered with marzipan and decorated with icing. In France, it is a *Bûche de Noël*, a chocolate log cake symbolizing the yule log, which was once kept burning throughout the 12 days of Christmas. The Italians make Panettone, a light sweet bread enriched with dried fruits, while the Germans enjoy Stollen, a yeast cake with dried fruit, sometimes stuffed with marzipan.

Nowadays, many people have a more modern take on Christmas foods. What about offering your visitors a Reindeer Cupcake or a Snow-covered Ginger Muffin? This book contains plenty of wonderful recipes for seasonal fare, from the truly traditional to those with a contemporary twist.

Family fun

Christmas preparations offer a great opportunity to get the whole family involved, regardless of age. The anticipation and preparation are often as enjoyable as the main event, and it's a good way to channel all that pre-Christmas excitement and get the kids to work off steam. Most families have their own traditions and it is these rituals, such as baking the same muffins every year, or decorating the Christmas tree, that make the fondest memories.

One reliable source of family fun is to make your own edible Christmas decorations. They look beautiful, they taste good, and they are fun to make. Even very small children can help cut out the cookie shapes or hang them up with ribbon. It also offers an opportunity for creative expression – even if you do end up with clashing colours and gaudy finishing touches. This is the one time of year when a bit of bad taste is acceptable and all part of the fun.

Baking biscuits for Santa is another lovely activity for keeping traditions and beliefs alive. Again, it is one where children can take an active role, and gives the adults something to nibble when the kids are in bed. Children can help make the biscuits, then put them on a plate and leave them out for Santa to enjoy when he delivers the gifts on the stroke of midnight. Don't forget to leave him a drink – milk, hot cocoa, cider, mulled wine – or something stronger...

Edible gifts

Everyone loves homemade biscuits and sweets, and they are always gratefully received as gifts at Christmas-time. People really appreciate the effort involved in making them, and they are usually far superior to their shop-bought counterparts. Consider mouth-watering biscuits such as Ginger Snowmen, Mulled Wine Biscuits and Sweet Biscotti. Or what about scrumptious sweets such as Chocolate Cherry Fudge, Marrons Glacés, Sugar Plums or Champagne Truffles?

Choosing attractive packaging for edible gifts is very important, and enjoyable too. Look out for pretty gift boxes and line them with tissue in matching colours to keep the biscuits or sweets from moving around and getting damaged. Alternatively, buy a roll of scrunchy cellophane and use to wrap the sweet treats, securing with invisible tape and festive ribbons and bows. If necessary, add a pretty tag with detailed storage instructions and a 'best before' date.

Christmas drinks

As well as all the traditional Christmas foods, there are seasonal drinks too. For the ultimate in comfort, curl up by the fire with a winter warmer such as Festive Hot Chocolate. This book also contains recipes for a range of tempting cold drinks, such as Cranberry Crush, which will be enjoyed by family and friends alike and is great for serving at parties.

Christmas traditions

Traditions and rituals vary around the Christian world as people celebrate Christmas in their different ways. Great Britain and the United States share many customs including carol singing and Christmas stockings. Another shared tradition is that of the Christmas tree, a custom that originated in Germany. Advent calendars also came from Germany. They used to consist of 24 little boxes hanging on a fir wreath, each containing a tiny gift, but nowadays they are more likely to be made of cardboard with little windows to open, counting down the days to Christmas Day.

The main focus of the festive period is Christmas dinner, usually served at lunchtime on Christmas Day. This is generally roast turkey, followed by mince pies and plum pudding. Traditionally the pudding was made a month before Christmas and every member of the family took a turn in stirring the mixture, while making a wish. Small silver coins or charms were hidden in the pudding, bringing luck to those who found one in their portion.

In France, the main celebration is held late on Christmas Eve, or in the early hours of Christmas morning after Mass. These days, turkey and chestnuts are popular, but many still prefer a goose. In the southeast, the meal always finished with the 13 Christmas desserts, symbolizing the 13 present at the Last Supper. These are *pompe à l'huile* (fruit pastry), raisins, quince paste, marzipan sweets, nougat, *fougasse* (rich cake), crystallized lemons, walnuts and hazelnuts, pears, plums, dried figs, almonds and dates.

Italians feast on Christmas Eve until after Midnight Mass, when they have a grand feast which often includes *cotechino*, a fresh pork sausage served with lentils. Traditional Dutch foods are carp, small spicy cakes called *spéculos*, apples, which represent the tree of knowledge, and nuts, symbolizing life's hardships, while Scandinavian festive foods include fruit-filled pastries and cakes, braised ham and marinated fish.

150 g (5 oz) **plain flour**

50 g (2 oz) **caster sugar**

1 teaspoon **ground ginger**

100 g (3½ oz) **butter**, cut into pieces

24 small **coloured balls** or **tiny sweets**

125 g (4 oz) ready-to-roll **white icing** or **marzipan (almond paste)**

pink and blue food colouring

small tube **black writing icing**

Icing:

125 g (4 oz) **icing sugar**

1 pinch **ground ginger**

5 teaspoons **water**

Makes 12
Preparation time: **30 minutes**
Cooking time: **7–8 minutes**

Ginger snowmen

These crisp shortbread biscuits flavoured with just a hint of ginger are sure to delight any young child.

1 Put the flour, sugar and ginger into a mixing bowl or a food processor. Add the butter and rub in with the fingertips or blend until the mixture resembles fine crumbs.

2 Continue mixing, or form the ingredients into a soft ball with your hands. Knead lightly, then roll out thinly between two pieces of nonstick baking paper.

3 Cut out snowmen shapes using a 10 cm (4 inch) cookie cutter and transfer to ungreased baking sheets. Bake the snowmen in a preheated oven, 180°C (350°F), Gas Mark 4, for 7–8 minutes until pale golden. Leave to cool on the baking sheets then transfer to a wire rack set over the sheets.

4 To make the icing, sift the icing sugar and ginger into a bowl. Gradually mix in the water until you have a smooth icing. Spoon over the biscuits and allow to drizzle over the edges. Position the silver balls for eyes, then leave to dry and harden.

5 To complete the decoration, colour half of the ready-to-roll icing pink and the other half blue. Roll out on a surface dusted with a little icing sugar and cut out strips for scarves. Drape the scarves around the snowmen's necks. Reroll the trimmings and cut semi-circles for the hats and shape small balls for the pompoms. Add to the snowmen, sticking the pompoms with a little water. Pipe on small, black, smiling mouths. Leave for 1 hour to harden before serving.

4 tablespoons **crunchy peanut butter**

100 g (3½ oz) **butter**, at room temperature

75 g (3 oz) **light muscovado sugar**

150 g (5 oz) **self-raising flour**

1–2 tablespoons **milk**

Makes 16
*Preparation time: **20 minutes***
*Cooking time: **8–10 minutes***

Peanut butter biscuits

These soft, buttery biscuits taste delicious warm from the oven. If you plan to leave some out for Santa, hide them from the rest of the family.

1 Lightly butter 2 baking sheets. Put the peanut butter, butter and sugar into a mixing bowl or a food processor and beat until smooth.

2 Mix in the flour and add enough milk to make a smooth dough. Use your hands to shape teaspoons of the mixture into balls and arrange them, spaced apart, on the prepared baking sheets.

3 Bake the biscuits in a preheated oven, 180°C (350°F), Gas Mark 4, for 8–10 minutes until cracked and golden. Allow them to harden for a minute or two, then transfer to a wire rack to cool. These biscuits are best eaten on the day they are made but can be stored in an airtight container for up to 4 days.

Mulled wine biscuits

With the warm, spicy flavours of mulled wine, these cookies make a great accompaniment to coffee – perfect for serving to friends and neighbours who drop in during the holidays.

1 Put the raisins and cranberries into a small heavy-based saucepan with the wine, redcurrrant jelly and spices. Heat until the jelly dissolves, then bring to the boil and boil for 2–3 minutes until the syrup is reduced by about half. Allow to cool.

2 Lightly grease a large baking sheet. Mix the nuts and chocolate in a bowl with the flour, orange rind, melted butter, egg and fruit mixture to make a paste. Place teaspoons of the mixture, spaced slightly apart, on the prepared baking sheet.

3 Bake the biscuits in a preheated oven, 180°C (350°F), Gas Mark 4, for about 20 minutes until they have spread slightly. Leave them on the baking sheet for 3 minutes, then transfer to a wire rack to cool. Dust generously with icing sugar. The biscuits can be stored in an airtight container for up to a week.

140 g (4½ oz) **raisins**

75 g (3 oz) **dried cranberries**

150 ml (¼ pint) **red wine**

100 g (3½ oz) **redcurrant jelly**

1 pinch **chilli powder**

1 teaspoon **ground cinnamon**

¼ teaspoon **ground cloves**

50 g (2 oz) **walnuts**, chopped

50 g (2 oz) **whole blanched almonds**, chopped

100 g (3½ oz) **plain dark chocolate**

75 g (3 oz) **self-raising flour**

finely grated rind of 1 **orange**

50 g (2 oz) **unsalted butter**, melted

1 **egg**

icing sugar, for dusting

Makes about 25
*Preparation time: **15 minutes***
*Cooking time: **25–30 minutes***

75 g (3 oz) **butter**

4 tablespoons **golden syrup**

100 g (3½ oz) **caster sugar**

1 teaspoon **ground cinnamon**

½ teaspoon **ground ginger**

1 large pinch **ground allspice**

300 g (10 oz) **plain flour**

1 teaspoon **bicarbonate of soda**

3 tablespoons **milk**

125 g (4 oz) **ready-to-pipe white icing**

a few **edible coloured balls**, (optional)

Makes 25
Preparation time: **40 minutes**
Cooking time: **15–17 minutes**

Tree decorations

The wonderful aroma of cinnamon, ginger and allspice that pervades the house while these festive biscuits are baking sums up the spirit of Christmas-time. This is a great activity for children to join in.

1 Lightly grease 3 baking sheets. Put the butter, syrup and sugar into a saucepan and heat gently, stirring occasionally, until the butter has melted and the sugar dissolved.

2 Take the pan off the heat and stir in the spices. Mix together the flour and bicarbonate of soda and then beat into the spicy butter mixture, adding enough milk to make a smooth dough.

3 Turn out the dough on to a board and leave for 5–10 minutes until it is cool enough to handle. Knead well then roll out on a floured surface or a piece of nonstick baking paper.

4 Cut out festive shapes using star, stocking, reindeer, Santa and bell-shaped cutters. Reroll the trimmings and cut out more shapes. Transfer the shapes to the prepared baking sheets.

5 Make a hole in the top of each biscuit with the end of a skewer or a teaspoon handle and bake in a preheated oven, 180°C (350°F), Gas Mark 4, for 10–12 minutes until browned. Enlarge the hole for ribbon if needed. Allow to cool on the baking sheets.

6 Pipe the icing on to the biscuits, add the coloured balls, if using, and let harden. Thread fine ribbons through the holes on the biscuits and tie on to the Christmas tree. Eat within 2 days.

TIP

If the children take a long time cutting out the biscuits, you may need to soften the dough in the microwave for about 20 seconds before rerolling.

150 g (5 oz) **butter**

200 g (7 oz) **caster sugar**

few drops of **vanilla extract**

1 **egg yolk**

1 tablespoon **milk**

1 generous pinch **ground cardamom**

1 generous pinch **ground cinnamon**

finely grated rind of ½ **lemon**

50 g (2 oz) **ground almonds**

175 g (6 oz) **plain flour**, sifted

125 g (4 oz) **plain dark chocolate**, chopped

Makes 15
*Preparation time: **20 minutes**, plus chilling*
*Cooking time: **15 minutes***

Sweet biscotti

These chocolate-dipped Italian biscuits make a pretty and sophisticated gift at Christmas. Pack in coloured cellophane bags and tie with ribbon.

1 Beat the butter in a mixing bowl with the sugar and vanilla extract until pale and creamy. Add the egg yolk, milk, spices, lemon rind and ground almonds and knead the sifted flour into this mixture. Chill in the refrigerator for 1 hour.

2 Form the dough into rectangular blocks, about 4 cm (1½ inches) in diameter, wrap in foil, and chill in the refrigerator for 2 hours.

3 Grease a baking sheet. Cut the blocks of dough into 5 mm (¼ inch) slices, place on the baking sheet and bake in a preheated oven, 190°C (375°F), Gas Mark 5, for 15 minutes. Remove the biscotti with a metal spatula and cool on a wire rack.

4 Place the chocolate in a heatproof bowl and melt over a pan of gently simmering water. Dip the biscotti into the chocolate so that they are half coated and allow to cool on nonstick baking paper. The biscotti can be stored in an airtight container for up to a week.

Chocolate hazelnut biscuits

Speckled with chunky pieces of hazelnut and diced chocolate, these dark chocolate biscuits are best served while they are still just warm from the oven – a real festive treat.

1 Grease 2 large baking sheets. Put the cocoa powder into a small bowl and mix to a smooth paste with the boiling water.

2 Cream the butter and sugars in a bowl until light and fluffy. Add the cocoa paste and a little of the egg and beat well. Mix together the flour and bicarbonate of soda then mix in alternately with the remaining egg.

3 Stir in the chopped chocolate and nuts. Drop teaspoons of the mixture, well spaced apart, on to the baking sheets. Bake the cookies in a preheated oven, 180°C (350°F), Gas Mark 4, for 8–10 minutes until golden. Allow to harden for a minute or two then transfer to a wire rack to cool. These cookies are best eaten soon after making but they can be stored in an airtight container for up to 4 days.

4 teaspoons **cocoa powder**

5 teaspoons **boiling water**

100 g (3½ oz) **butter**, at room temperature

75 g (3 oz) **light muscovado sugar**

75 g (3 oz) **caster sugar**

1 **egg**, beaten

150 g (5 oz) **plain flour**

½ teaspoon **bicarbonate of soda**

100 g (3½ oz) **plain dark chocolate**, finely diced

75 g (3 oz) **blanched hazelnuts**, chopped

Makes 24
*Preparation time: **30 minutes***
*Cooking time: **8–10 minutes***

100 g (3½ oz) **butter**

6 tablespoons **maple syrup**

50 g (2 oz) **caster sugar**

1 teaspoon **bicarbonate of soda**

1 **egg yolk**

150 g (5 oz) **plain flour**

¼ teaspoon **ground cinnamon**

75 g (3 oz) **plain dark chocolate**, broken into pieces

75 g (3 oz) **white chocolate**, broken into pieces

Makes 40
*Preparation time: **20 minutes**, plus setting*
*Cooking time: **12–15 minutes***

Maple biscuits

Dipped in chocolate, these delectable maple biscuits are thin and crisp. Serve with coffee or hot chocolate for a mid-morning treat.

1 Melt the butter in a saucepan, then let it cool slightly.

2 Stir the maple syrup, caster sugar, bicarbonate of soda, and egg yolk into the melted butter then mix in the flour and cinnamon. Beat until you have a smooth creamy dough.

3 Drop teaspoons of the mixture, spaced slightly apart, on a baking sheet lined with nonstick baking paper. Bake the biscuits in a preheated oven, 190°C (375°F), Gas Mark 5, for 4–5 minutes until golden brown. Let them harden for a minute or two then transfer to a wire rack using a metal spatula. Continue until all the mixture has been used.

4 Place the plain chocolate in one heatproof bowl and the white chocolate in another. Set them over pans of gently simmering water and allow to melt.

5 Hold one of the biscuits over the bowl and spoon a little of the chocolate over half of it, spreading it with the back of the spoon. Return the biscuit to the wire rack and coat all the biscuits in the same way. Leave in a cool place for 30 minutes until the chocolate has hardened then pack into an airtight container, separating the layers with sheets of nonstick or greaseproof paper. The biscuits can be stored for up to 2 days.

TIPS
For a change, use honey instead of maple syrup, or ground ginger in place of cinnamon. Try sprinkling brown sugar over the biscuits just before cooking, instead of coating them in chocolate.

200 g (7 oz) **unsalted butter**, at room temperature

100 g (3½ oz) **caster sugar**

200 g (7 oz) **plain flour**

½ teaspoon **baking powder**

25 g (1 oz) **cocoa powder**

2 teaspoons **milk**

100 g (3½ oz) **plain dark chocolate**, broken into pieces

Makes 12
*Preparation time: **15 minutes***
*Cooking time: **15–20 minutes***

Chocolate Viennese whirls

A chocolate version of buttery little Viennese whirls, these little cookies are set in pretty cake cases and filled with melted chocolate after baking.

1 Line a 12-section tarlet tin with paper cake cases. Beat together the butter and sugar until pale and creamy. Sift the flour, baking powder and cocoa powder into the bowl, add the milk and beat well to make a smooth paste.

2 Spoon the mixture into a piping bag fitted with a large star nozzle and pipe swirls into the paper cases, leaving a large hole in the centre.

3 Bake the whirls in a preheated oven, 190°C (375°F), Gas Mark 5, for 15–20 minutes or until slightly risen. Press a hole in the centre of each one. Allow to cool in the tin.

4 To decorate, place the chocolate in a heatproof bowl and melt over a saucepan of gently simmering water. Spoon a little chocolate into the centre of each whirl. Allow to set slightly before serving.

Chocolate macaroons

Crisp on the outside and moist inside, little chocolate macaroons make a stylish accompaniment to coffee after Christmas dinner.

1 Line a large baking sheet with nonstick baking paper. Whisk the egg whites until stiff, then gradually whisk in the sugar until the mixture is thick and glossy. Gently fold in the ground almonds and grated chocolate.

2 Put the mixture into a large piping bag fitted with a large plain nozzle and pipe small rounds, about 4 cm ($1\frac{1}{2}$ inches) in diameter, on to the baking sheet. Alternatively, place small teaspoons of dough on the baking sheet.

3 Press a chocolate-covered coffee bean into the centre of each macaroon. Bake in a preheated oven, 190°C (375°F), Gas Mark 5, for about 15 minutes until slightly risen and just firm. Leave the macaroons on the paper to cool. Store in an airtight container.

TIP
Chocolate-covered coffee beans are available from some supermarkets and coffee specialists. If you can't find them, decorate each macaroon with a whole blanched almond.

2 **egg whites**

100 g (3½ oz) **caster sugar**

125 g (4 oz) **ground almonds**

50 g (2 oz) **plain dark chocolate**, grated

25 **chocolate-covered coffee beans**, to decorate

Makes 25
*Preparation time: **10 minutes***
*Cooking time: **15 minutes***

100 g (3½ oz) **butter**, at room temperature

4 tablespoons **golden syrup**

75 g (3 oz) **light muscovado sugar**

75 g (3 oz) **plain flour**

½ teaspoon **bicarbonate of soda**

1 teaspoon **ground ginger**

75 g (3 oz) **rolled oats**, plus extra for sprinkling

Makes 20
*Preparation time: **20 minutes***
*Cooking time: **8–10 minutes***

Oatmeal biscuits

This is a comforting, old-fashioned biscuit that keeps well and is ideal to have on hand for unexpected guests.

1 Lightly grease 2 baking sheets. Put the butter, syrup and sugar into a bowl and beat until light and creamy.

2 Mix the flour with the bicarbonate of soda and ginger, then gradually beat it into the creamed mixture. Stir in the oats.

3 Drop heaped teaspoonfuls of the biscuit mixture, spaced well apart, on the greased baking sheets. Sprinkle with a few extra oats and cook in a preheated oven, 180°C (350°F), Gas Mark 4, for 8–10 minutes until golden.

4 Let the biscuits harden for a minute or two, then transfer them to a wire rack to cool. They can be stored in an airtight container for up to 4 days.

Linzer biscuits

These rich hazelnut shortbreads have a just a hint of lemon and a raspberry jam filling. Tiny heart and star-shaped cutters can be used to cut out the centres of the biscuits.

1 Grind the hazelnuts very finely in a blender or coffee grinder.

2 Put the flour and sugar into a mixing bowl or a food processor, add the butter and rub in with your fingertips or process until the mixture forms fine crumbs.

3 Stir in the ground hazelnuts and lemon rind, then mix in the egg yolk and bring the mixture together with your hands to form a firm dough.

4 Knead the dough lightly on a work surface dusted with a little flour. Roll out half the dough to 1 cm (¹/₂ inch) thickness and cut out 5.5 cm (2¹/₄ inch) rounds with a fluted cutter. Arrange on an ungreased baking sheet. Use a biscuit cutter to remove 2.5 cm (1 inch) hearts and stars from the centres of half of the biscuits.

5 Bake the first batch of biscuits in a preheated oven, 160°C (350°F), Gas Mark 3, for about 8 minutes, until pale golden brown. Meanwhile, roll out the second half of the dough and cut shapes as before. Reroll the trimmings, cutting out shapes until all the dough has been used, and bake as before. Leave the cookies on the baking sheets for a minute or two to harden, then transfer to a wire rack to cool.

6 Divide the jam between the centres of the whole biscuits and spread thickly, leaving a border of biscuit showing. Cover with the hole-cut biscuits, dust with a little sifted icing sugar and leave to cool completely before serving.

50 g (2 oz) **hazelnuts**

225 g (7½ oz) **plain flour**

75 g (3 oz) **caster sugar**

150 g (5 oz) **butter**, cut into pieces

finely grated rind of ½ **lemon**

1 **egg yolk**

4 tablespoons **seedless raspberry jam**

icing sugar, to decorate

Makes 16
*Preparation time: **35 minutes***
*Cooking time: **16 minutes***

225 g (7½ oz) **strong white bread flour**

1 teaspoon **fast action dried yeast**

2 teaspoons **caster sugar**

large pinch of **salt**

15 g (½ oz) melted **butter** or **sunflower oil**

100 ml (3½ fl oz) **warm water**

75 g (3 oz) each **plain dark**, **white** and **milk chocolate**, broken into pieces

Glaze:

2 tablespoons **water**

½ teaspoon **salt**

Makes 40
*Preparation time: **30 minutes**, plus rising and setting*
*Cooking time: **6–8 minutes***

Triple chocolate pretzels

These dainty bread morsels are brushed with their traditional salt glaze before baking, and then drizzled with dark, white and milk chocolate to make eye-catching petits fours.

1 Lightly grease 2 large baking sheets.

2 Mix the flour, yeast, sugar and salt in a bowl. Add the melted butter or oil and gradually mix in the warm water until you have a smooth dough. Knead the dough for 5 minutes on a lightly floured surface until smooth and elastic.

3 Cut the dough into quarters, then cut each quarter into 10 smaller pieces. Shape each piece into a thin rope about 20 cm (8 inches) long. Bend the rope so that it forms a wide arc, then bring one of the ends round in a loop and secure about halfway along the rope. Do the same with the other end, looping it across the first secured end.

4 Transfer the pretzels to the greased baking sheets. Cover loosely with lightly oiled clingfilm and leave in a warm place for 30 minutes until well risen.

5 To make the glaze, mix the water and salt in a bowl until the salt has dissolved then brush this over the pretzels. Bake in a preheated oven, 200°C (400°F), Gas Mark 6, for 6–8 minutes until golden brown. Transfer to a wire rack and leave to cool.

6 Place the dark, white and milk chocolates in 3 separate heatproof bowls and melt over pans of gently simmering water. Using a spoon, drizzle random lines of dark chocolate over the pretzels. Leave to harden then repeat with the white and then the milk chocolate. When set, transfer to an airtight container and eat within 2 days.

500 g (1 lb) **granulated sugar**

350 ml (12 fl oz) **water**

2 tablespoons **golden syrup**

25 g (1 oz) **butter**

125 ml (4 fl oz) **double cream**

50 g (2 oz) **plain dark chocolate**, broken into pieces

100 g (3½ oz) **glacé cherries**, roughly chopped

Makes 30 squares
*Preparation time: **10 minutes***
*Cooking time: **15–17 minutes***

Chocolate cherry fudge

This rich dark chocolate fudge, speckled with vibrant red glacé cherries, looks festive and tastes delicious too. It makes a great stocking filler, or an ideal gift for school friends.

1 Put the sugar, water and syrup into a heavy-based saucepan and heat gently, without stirring, until the sugar has dissolved. Meanwhile, lightly grease an 18 cm (7 inch) shallow cake tin with a little butter.

2 Put a sugar thermometer into the pan and increase the heat. Cook until the thermometer reads 110°C (225°F). Stir in half of the cream and heat for 2–3 minutes until the temperature reaches 115°C (238°F).

3 Mix in the remaining cream and heat for about 5 minutes until the temperature reaches 116–118°C (240–245°F) or a little of the syrup forms a soft ball when dropped into cold water. Keep a watchful eye over the fudge as it cooks. Stir more frequently as the heat increases so that the fudge does not burn.

4 Take the pan off the heat, let it cool for 2–3 minutes then add the chocolate and the remaining butter. Stir constantly for 3–4 minutes until the chocolate and butter have melted and the fudge begins to thicken and look grainy. Stir in the cherries then pour the mixture into the prepared cake tin. Let the fudge cool for 10 minutes then mark it into squares and leave to cool completely.

5 Loosen the edges of the fudge from the sides of the tin, turn it out on to a chopping board and cut into small squares. Wrap in squares of coloured cellophane and tie with ribbon or raffia. The fudge can be stored for up to 1 week.

Creamy pistachio toffee

This golden toffee is made with rich double cream and green pistachios. Break it into pieces and pack in pretty jars or coloured cellophane to make an attractive gift.

300 g (10 oz) **granulated sugar**

300 ml (½ pint) **double cream**

25 g (1 oz) **butter**

50 g (2 oz) **pistachio nuts**, roughly chopped

Makes 30 pieces
*Preparation time: **15 minutes***
*Cooking time: **20 minutes***

1 Put the sugar and cream into a heavy-based saucepan and heat gently, stirring occasionally, until the sugar has completely dissolved. Meanwhile, use a little of the butter to grease an 18 cm (7 inch) shallow square cake tin.

2 Stir the remaining butter into the sugar and cream mixture, add a sugar thermometer if you have one, and increase the heat. Cook for about 15 minutes until the temperature reaches 120°C (250°F) or a little of the toffee forms a hard ball when dropped into a bowl of cold water. Stir the toffee occasionally at first, then more frequently as the mixture begins to colour and thicken so that it cooks to an even creamy brown and doesn't burn on the bottom of the saucepan.

3 As you continue to heat, the toffee will froth then thicken with a grainy texture. When the butter begins to separate out of the toffee, it is almost ready. Cook for a few more minutes until it changes to a smooth glossy toffee.

4 Take the pan off the heat, quickly stir in the pistachio nuts, then pour the toffee into the buttered tin. Allow to cool for 5 minutes then mark into strips and leave to cool completely.

5 When cold, loosen the edges of the toffee from the sides of the tin and turn it out. Break into pieces with a toffee hammer or by hitting a cook's knife with a rolling pin. Wrap pieces of toffee in coloured cellophane and tie with thin ribbon or raffia. It can be stored for up to 1 week.

150 g (5 oz) **mixed whole nuts**, such as **cashews, hazelnuts, pistachios**

300 g (10 oz) **plain dark chocolate**, broken into pieces

15 g (½ oz) **butter**

2 tablespoons **icing sugar**

2 tablespoons **double cream**

Makes 28
*Preparation time: **40 minutes**,*
plus chilling and setting
*Cooking time: **10 minutes***

Rocky road clusters

Pistachios, cashews and hazelnuts are toasted then coated in dark chocolate to create appealing nut clusters. The jagged shapes look particularly attractive when packed into a mixed box of petits fours.

1 Put the nuts on a piece of foil on a baking sheet, then toast under a preheated hot grill for 3–4 minutes until golden. Allow to cool slightly then chop roughly.

2 Meanwhile, place 75 g (3 oz) of the chocolate in a heatproof bowl and melt over a pan of gently simmering water. Stir the butter, sugar and cream into the melted chocolate until smooth and glossy, then mix in all but 2 tablespoons of the chopped nuts.

3 Drop rough teaspoons of the mixture on to a baking sheet lined with nonstick baking paper. Chill for 2–3 hours until firm.

4 To finish, melt the remaining chocolate as before. Coat the nut clusters in the melted chocolate by holding them on a fork, one at a time, over the bowl of chocolate and spooning some of it over the top with a teaspoon. When the excess chocolate has dripped away, return the cluster to the paper-lined tray and repeat with the remainder.

5 Put the chocolates in a cool place and leave to set for at least an hour. Sprinkle with the reserved nuts. Transfer them to petit four cases when ready to serve.

TIP
Nuts burn quickly, so don't leave them unattended while toasting.

Champagne truffles

For the ultimate chocolate experience, bite through a brittle chocolate coating to a soft creamy Champagne centre.

1 Place half of the dark chocolate in a heatproof bowl and melt over a saucepan of gently simmering water. Stir in the Champagne or sparkling wine, the cream and the sugar and mix until smooth and glossy. Chill for 4–5 hours or overnight.

2 Using 2 teaspoons, scoop and scrape the soft truffle mixture into rough balls and arrange on a plate. Freeze for 30 minutes to harden.

3 Put the cocoa powder on a saucer and, dipping your fingertips in it regularly, roll the truffles into neat rounds. Return to the plate and freeze again until firm.

4 Melt the remaining dark chocolate as before. Coat the truffles with the melted chocolate by holding them on a fork, one at a time, over the bowl of chocolate and using a teaspoon to spoon the chocolate over the top. When the excess chocolate has dripped away, place the truffles on a baking sheet lined with nonstick baking paper.

5 Chill the truffles for 1 hour until hardened. Melt the white chocolate as before and drizzle or pipe the truffles with white lines. Chill again until the decoration has hardened, then transfer to petit four cases. Arrange the truffles in a small box; they can be stored in the refrigerator for up to 5 days.

300 g (10 oz) **plain dark chocolate**, broken into pieces

125 ml (4 fl oz) **Champagne** or **sparkling dry white wine**

3 tablespoons **double cream**

2 tablespoons **icing sugar**

2 teaspoons **cocoa powder**

50 g (2 oz) **white chocolate**, broken into pieces

Makes 20
*Preparation time: **45 minutes**, plus chilling and freezing*
*Cooking time: **10 minutes***

125 ml (4 fl oz) **double cream**

150 g (5 oz) **white chocolate**,
broken into pieces

25 g (1 oz) **strong**, **hard
white peppermints**

40 g (1½ oz) **icing sugar**

Makes 20
*Preparation time: **30 minutes**,*
plus chilling
*Cooking time: **4–5 minutes***

White chocolate mint truffles

**Smooth white chocolate truffles lightly flavoured with crushed peppermints
are perfect for an after-dinner sweet.**

1 Pour the cream into a heavy-based saucepan and add the chocolate. Heat gently, stirring occasionally, for 4–5 minutes until the chocolate has melted. Allow to cool.

2 Whisk the cream mixture until thick, then chill in the refrigerator for 3–4 hours.

3 Put the peppermints into a plastic bag, crush with a rolling pin then stir into the chilled cream mixture. Drop teaspoons of the soft mixture on to a plate and chill for 1 hour or freeze for 30 minutes until firm.

4 Sprinkle the icing sugar on another plate, then roll the truffles in the sugar to form neat balls. Pack into a small box lined with greaseproof paper and dust with the remaining sugar. Chill for at least 2 hours before serving. The truffles can be stored in the refrigerator for up to 4 days.

VARIATION
Roll the truffles in grated white chocolate instead of the icing sugar. Alternatively, coat them in a solid chocolate shell (see Champagne Truffles on page 29).

300 g (10 oz) **plain dark chocolate**, broken into pieces

225 g (7½ oz) **strawberries**

125 g (4 oz) **red cherries** or **grapes**

50 g (2 oz) **Brazil nuts**

Serves 4
*Preparation time: **25 minutes**, plus chilling*
*Cooking time: **10 minutes***

Chocolate fruit cups

Little chocolate cases make tempting and impressive containers for dainty fruit and nut treats.

1 Place two-thirds of the chocolate pieces in a heatproof bowl and melt over a saucepan of gently simmering water.

2 Cut out 4 circles of heavy-duty foil, about 20 cm (8 inches) in diameter. Take 1 circle and mould it around an orange or a large apple, fitting it tightly around the base of the fruit and pulling up the edges of the foil to create a cup shape. Carefully remove the fruit and press the foil cup gently on a work surface to make a flat base. Shape the remaining foil circles in the same way.

3 Spoon a little chocolate into one of the foil cups, then spread it around the inside with the back of the spoon. Coat the remaining cups in the same way, using about half the chocolate. Chill for about 10 minutes until beginning to set, then give the cups a second coat with the remaining melted chocolate. Chill for at least 30 minutes until set.

4 Meanwhile, melt the remaining chocolate as before. Half-dip the fruit and nuts in the chocolate and leave to set on a sheet of greaseproof paper.

5 Use cool hands to peel the foil away from the chocolate cups, starting at the top and working down to the bottom. Fill the cups with the fruit and nuts and keep in a cool place until ready to serve.

Caramelized pecans

Here, pecan nuts are sandwiched with a layer of moist hazelnut marzipan, then coated in a glass-like golden caramel for a professional finish that is easy to obtain at home.

1 Place the hazelnuts on a baking sheet and grill under a preheated grill until lightly browned. Allow to cool slightly, then grind finely in a food processor or blender. Brush a baking sheet with a little oil.

2 Reconstitute the egg white with warm water, according to the packet instructions, then add the caster sugar and ground hazelnuts and mix to a stiff paste.

3 Sandwich the pecan nuts together in pairs with a little of the hazelnut marzipan in between.

4 Put the granulated sugar and water into a heavy-based saucepan and heat gently, without stirring, until the sugar has completely dissolved. Increase the heat and cook for 10–15 minutes until the syrup has turned golden.

5 Plunge the base of the pan into a bowl of cold water to prevent the syrup from cooking and darkening further. Drop the sandwiched pecan nuts, one at a time, into the caramel. Lift out with a fork and place on the oiled baking sheet.

6 Let the pecans cool and harden, then transfer them to petit four cases. They can be stored in an airtight container for up to 4 days. Separate the layers with greaseproof paper.

TIP
If the caramelized nuts are left uncovered the moisture in the air, especially in a hot steamy kitchen, will soften the coating.

50 g (2 oz) blanched **hazelnuts**

oil, for brushing

1 dried **egg white**

50 g (2 oz) **caster sugar**

125 g (4 oz) **pecan nuts**

225 g (7 oz) **granulated sugar**

65 ml (2½ fl oz) **water**

Makes 35
*Preparation time: **40 minutes***
*Cooking time: **20 minutes***

500 g (1 lb) **fresh chestnuts**

200 g (3½ oz) **granulated sugar**

250 ml (8 fl oz) **liquid glucose**

250 ml (8 fl oz) **water**

½ teaspoon **vanilla extract**

To finish:

100 g (3½ oz) **granulated sugar**

3 tablespoons **water**

Makes 60
*Preparation time: **40 minutes**,*
*plus standing, **over 10 days***
*Cooking time: **35 minutes***

Marrons glacés

These French favourites are wonderful served with coffee after a meal or used to decorate chocolate desserts and ice creams.

1 Make a small cross-cut in the top of each chestnut shell, then boil for 2 minutes. Peel away the shell and the inner skin with a small knife. If the nuts are hard to peel, return them to the pan, bring back to the boil and try again.

2 Put the peeled chestnuts into a pan, cover with cold water, bring to the boil and simmer gently for 20 minutes until just tender. Drain and transfer to a shallow dish.

3 To make a sugar syrup, put the sugar, liquid glucose and water into a saucepan. Heat gently until the sugar has dissolved, then boil for 1 minute. Pour over the chestnuts, cover with a plate and leave in a warm place overnight.

4 On day 2, drain the syrup into a saucepan and boil for 4 minutes. Pour over the chestnuts, cover and leave overnight as before. On day 3, repeat as on day 2, adding the vanilla extract after boiling. On day 4, repeat the sugar boiling process once more. Add the chestnuts, then soak for 3 days.

5 On day 7, arrange the chestnuts in a layer on a wire rack set over a baking sheet. Leave in a warm place for 2–3 days, turning once or twice until the coating is hard.

6 On day 9 or 10, make the glacé finish. Boil some water in a pan. Put the sugar and water in another pan. Heat until the sugar has dissolved, then boil for 1 minute. Using tongs, dip the chestnuts into the boiling water. Shake off the excess moisture then dip into the sugar syrup. Dry the chestnuts overnight on a rack. Wrap in foil and store in an airtight container. They will keep for 3 months.

Sugar plums

These traditional Christmas-time sweets are made with moist chopped dates, sultanas, prunes and cherries and flavoured with a little orange rind and brandy. Omit the alcohol if serving the sugar plums to children.

1 Put all the fruits into a food processor or blender and chop finely. Gradually work in the icing sugar, orange rind and brandy or orange juice until the mixture binds together. If you do not have a food processor, finely chop the fruits and mix in a bowl with the sugar, orange rind, brandy or juice.

2 Drop spoonfuls of the mixture on to a baking sheet, then roll them between your fingertips to shape into balls. If the mixture seems sticky at this stage, leave it for an hour for the fruits to absorb the brandy or orange juice, then try again.

3 Allow the sugar plums to dry at room temperature for 5–6 hours, then roll them in the caster sugar and arrange in petit four cases. Store in an airtight container at room temperature and eat within 3 days.

TIP
If you like nuts, substitute 1 cup of the fruit for some chunky, roughly chopped almonds, pistachios or hazelnuts.

150 g (5 oz) **chopped dates**

150 g (5 oz) **sultanas** or **raisins**

200 g (7 oz) **ready-to-eat stoned prunes**

200 g (7 oz) **glacé cherries**, halved

75 g (3 oz) **icing sugar**

finely grated rind of 1 **orange**

2 tablespoons **brandy** or **orange juice**

50 g (2 oz) **caster sugar**

Makes 32
*Preparation time: **20 minutes**, plus drying*

½ bunch **green seedless grapes**

½ bunch **red seedless grapes**

125 g (4 oz) **icing sugar**

4–5 teaspoons **orange** or **lime juice**

50 g (2 oz) **caster sugar**

Serves 6–8

*Preparation time: **20 minutes**, plus setting*

Frosted grapes

Complete a special meal and impress friends and family with this dainty dish of frosted fruit. They are quick and easy to make and even young children can help out.

1 Wash the grapes then pat dry with kitchen paper. Snip into tiny bunches of 2 or 3 grapes.

2 Sift the icing sugar into a bowl, then gradually mix in the fruit juice to make a smooth, thick frosting.

3 Dip the grapes, a bunch at a time, into the frosting then arrange them on a wire rack set over a baking sheet. Leave in a cool place for 1 hour or until hardened.

4 Sprinkle the grapes with the caster sugar then transfer to petit four cases or arrange on a plate. Eat within 3 days.

TIP
Fresh stemmed cherries and physalis may also be dipped in the frosting.

Panettone

Panettone is a traditional part of Christmas fare in Italy. This sweet, fruited yeast cake keeps well in an airtight container and can be reheated whole.

375g (12 oz) **plain flour**

1 large pinch of **salt**

1½ teaspoons **fast-action dried yeast**

50 g (2 oz) **caster sugar**

4 tablespoons **warm water**

3 **eggs** or 6 **egg yolks**

¼ teaspoon **vanilla extract**

2 teaspoons **finely grated lemon rind**

125 g (4 oz) **butter**, softened

75 g (3 oz) **sultanas**

3 tablespoons **candied citron peel**, chopped

25 g (1 oz) **melted butter**, for brushing

Serves 6–8
Preparation time: **30 minutes**, *plus rising*
Cooking time: **about 50 minutes**

1 Grease and line a 18 cm (7 inch) round cake tin. Sift 250 g (8 oz) of the flour and salt into a mixing bowl and leave in a warm place. Dissolve the yeast and 1 teaspoon of the sugar in the warm water and leave to froth.

2 Mix the remaining sugar into the flour. Beat the eggs with the vanilla extract and lemon rind. Stir in the flour, a third at a time, and mix into a soft dough which can be gathered into a ball. Gradually beat in the butter. Add a little more flour, working the dough with your hands into a manageable ball.

3 Turn out the dough on to a floured board and knead for about 10 minutes until smooth and silky, then put it into a warm bowl, cover and leave for 45–50 minutes, or until doubled in size.

4 Punch down the dough and knead in the sultanas and candied peel. Shape the dough into a ball, put it into the prepared tin and cut a cross in the top. Leave in a warm place for 15–20 minutes or until doubled in size.

5 Brush the top of the panettone with melted butter and bake in a preheated oven, 200°C (400°F), Gas Mark 6, for 10 minutes. Brush again with melted butter, reduce the oven temperature to 180°C (350°F), Gas Mark 4 and cook for another 40 minutes. The panettone is ready when the top is crisp and golden and a skewer inserted into the centre comes out clean. Cool on a wire rack. Serve cut into thick wedges.

Stollen

Traditionally served at Christmas, this German yeast cake is quite delicious. It is a slow riser because of the large amount of fruit but well worth the time it takes to make.

1 Blend the yeast in the warm water. Dissolve 50 g (2 oz) of the sugar and the salt in the milk. Add the rum, almond extract and yeast liquid.

2 Sift the flour into a bowl, making a well in the centre. Add the yeast mix, egg and half the softened butter cut into small pieces. Mix to a soft dough and knead for 10 minutes by hand, or 4–5 minutes in a large electric mixer fitted with a dough hook. Add the fruit and nuts.

3 Return the dough to the bowl, cover with a damp cloth and leave to rise in a warm place until doubled in size – about 2 hours.

4 Punch down the dough and knead until smooth, then roll it out on a lightly floured surface to a rectangle about 30 x 20 cm (12 x 8 inches).

5 Melt the remaining butter and brush liberally over the dough, then sprinkle with the remaining sugar. Shape the marzipan into a sausage the length of the rolled-out dough and add to the centre of the dough.

6 Fold one long side over just beyond the centre, and then fold over the other long side to overlap the first piece well. Press together lightly and slightly taper the ends.

7 Place the loaf on a greased baking sheet, brush with melted butter and leave in a warm place until almost doubled in size.

8 Bake the stollen in a preheated oven, 190°C (375°F), Gas Mark 5, for about 45 minutes. Cool on a wire rack. To serve, dredge heavily with icing sugar and cut into thin slices.

25 g (1 oz) **fresh yeast** or 15 g (½ oz) **fast action yeast**

2 tablespoons **warm water**

75 g (3 oz) **caster sugar**

1 pinch of **salt**

90 ml (3 fl oz) **warm milk**

2 tablespoons **rum**

a few drops of **almond extract**

425 g (14 oz) **plain flour**

1 **egg**, beaten

150 g (5 oz) **butter**, softened

50 g (2 oz) **raisins**

50 g (2 oz) **glacé cherries**, rinsed, dried and chopped

50 g (2 oz) **currants**

25 g (1 oz) **angelica**, chopped

50 g (2 oz) **cut mixed peel**

40 g (1½ oz) **flaked almonds**

175 g (6 oz) **marzipan**

sifted icing sugar, to serve

Serves 6
*Preparation time: **30 minutes**, plus rising*
*Cooking time: **45 minutes***

300 g (10 oz) **unsalted butter**

200 g (7 oz) **caster sugar**

3 large **eggs**, beaten

425 g (14 oz) **self-raising flour**

250 g (8 oz) **pineapple rings in syrup**

75 g (3 oz) **glacé cherries**, chopped

50 g (2 oz) **chopped mixed peel**

3 tablespoons **chopped angelica**

3 tablespoons **chopped walnuts**

3 tablespoons **desiccated coconut**

75 g (3 oz) **sultanas**

2 tablespoons **toasted coconut shavings**, to decorate

Icing

45 g (1½ oz) **unsalted butter**

250 g (8 oz) **icing sugar**

2 tablespoons **desiccated coconut**

Serves 10
*Preparation time: **30 minutes***
*Cooking time: **1¼–1½ hours***

Tropical Christmas cake

Bursting with colour and flavour, this tropical fruit cake makes for an original alternative to traditional Christmas fare.

1 Grease and flour a 23 cm (9 inch) ring mould or a 20 cm (8 inch) cake tin.

2 Cream the butter and sugar until soft and light. Gradually beat in the eggs. Sift the flour and fold into the creamed mixture.

3 Drain the canned pineapple, setting aside 1 tablespoon of the syrup for the icing and 3 tablespoons of the syrup for the cake. Chop the pineapple rings finely. Fold the dried fruit, nuts and pineapple into the cake mixture with the coconut, sultanas and the 3 tablespoons of pineapple syrup.

4 Put the mixture into the ring mould or cake tin. Bake in a preheated oven, 160°C (325°F), Gas Mark 3, for 1¼ hours if using a ring mould and 1½ hours if using a cake tin. Allow the cake to cool for at least 10 minutes in the tin, then turn out on to a wire rack and leave to cool completely.

5 To make the icing, melt the butter in a saucepan and then remove from the heat. Sift the icing sugar into the butter, then add 1 tablespoon of pineapple syrup and the coconut. Stir to combine, then spread the icing over the top of the cake and a little down the sides. Sprinkle with toasted coconut shavings.

3 **eggs**

75 g (3 oz) **icing sugar**, plus extra for sprinkling

50 g (2 oz) **plain flour**

25 g (1 oz) **cocoa powder**

150 ml (¼ pint) **double cream**

150 g (5 oz) **canned sweetened chestnut purée**

To decorate:

150 ml (¼ pint) **double cream**

200 g (7 oz) **plain dark chocolate**, broken into pieces

3 **chocolate flakes**

icing sugar, for dusting

Serves 10

*Preparation time: **40 minutes**, plus cooling*

*Cooking time: **20 minutes***

Bûche de Noël

Chocolate flakes give this French Yule log an authentic-looking bark. The log can be made a day in advance or it can be frozen. Dust with icing sugar just before serving.

1 Grease a 33 x 23 cm (13 x 19 inch) Swiss roll tin and line it with nonstick baking paper. Whisk the eggs and sugar in a heatproof bowl over a pan of hot water until the mixture leaves a trail when the beaters are lifted. Sift in the flour and cocoa powder and fold in with a metal spoon.

2 Pour the mixture into the prepared tin and spread it into the corners. Bake in a preheated oven, 180°C (350°F), Gas Mark 4, for about 15 minutes until just firm. Sprinkle a sheet of nonstick baking paper with icing sugar and invert the cake on to it. Peel away the paper that lined the tin, then roll the sponge in the fresh paper and leave to cool.

3 To make the filling, whip the cream until softly peaking, then fold in the chestnut purée. Unroll the sponge and spread the chestnut cream over the top. (Don't worry if the cake cracks, because the cracks won't show once the log is assembled.) Roll the cake back into a log shape.

4 To make the decoration, bring the cream almost to the boil in a small saucepan. Remove from the heat and stir in the chocolate pieces. Leave until melted, then stir until smooth. Allow to cool.

5 Arrange the cake, seam side down, on a serving plate. Lightly whip the chocolate cream, then spread it over the top and sides of the cake. Cut the flakes lengthwise into long pieces. Press them lightly on to the chocolate cream, filling in the gaps with smaller pieces of flake. To serve, dust the log liberally with icing sugar.

Cherub cake

This elegant layered cake is sandwiched with creamy butter and jam and flavoured with lime.

1 Line the base and sides of a 20 cm (8 inch) deep, round cake tin with nonstick baking paper. Cream the margarine and sugar until light and fluffy. Beat in the eggs and flour alternately until smooth.

2 Stir in the lime rind and the juice from half a lime. Spoon into the prepared tin and level. Bake in a preheated oven, 170°C (325°F), Gas Mark 3, for 1–1¼ hours until well risen. Cool in the tin then turn out; peel off the paper and slice into three layers.

3 Beat the butter, icing sugar and remaining lime juice until smooth. Sandwich cakes with butter cream and jam. Spread the remaining butter cream over top and sides.

4 Drape the rolled icing over the cake. Gently press over the top and sides until smooth, using your

fingertips dusted with a little icing sugar. Trim excess.

5 Shape a small piece of modelling icing into a ball and press into a 6 cm (2½ inch) nonstick cherub icing mould. Invert the mould and gently ease the shaped cherub out. Trim off excess icing. Transfer to a baking sheet lined with nonstick baking paper. Continue until 8 cherubs have been made.

6 Roll out the remaining icing, then cut thin strips. Twist each one into a corkscrew, propping up the twists with pieces of crumpled foil. Leave overnight to dry.

7 Paint gold detail on cherub wings. Arrange on top of the cake, with the icing ribbons. Secure with a little water or white frosting from a tube. Add fabric ribbon to side.

175 g (6 oz) **soft margarine**

175 g (6 oz) **caster sugar**

3 **eggs**

275 g (9 oz) **self-raising flour**

finely grated rind of 2 **limes**

juice of 1½ **limes**

100 g (3½ oz) **butter**, at room temperature

250 g (8 oz) **icing sugar**, plus extra for dusting

4 tablespoons **raspberry jam**

450 g (14½ oz) ready-to-roll **white icing**

250 g (8 oz) **modelling icing**

edible **gold food colouring**

Serves 8
*Preparation time: **1½ hours***
*Cooking time: **1–1¼ hours***

100 g (3½ oz) **fresh cranberries**

2 tablespoons **caster sugar**

1 large **pear**, peeled and sliced

thick **cranberry sauce**, to serve

Cake:

175 g (6 oz) **butter**, at room temperature

175 g (6 oz) **caster sugar**

3 **eggs**

200 g (7 oz) **self-raising flour**

finely grated rind of 1 **orange**

2 tablespoons **orange juice**

Serves 6–8
*Preparation time: **30 minutes***
*Cooking time: **1–1¼ hours***

Cranberry and pear upside-down cake

This is an ideal cake to make over the Christmas holidays, because it can be served warm with custard as a dessert, then cold the next day with coffee or tea.

1 Grease a 20 cm (8 inch) round springform tin and line with a circle of nonstick baking paper. Sprinkle the cranberries and sugar over the base then arrange the pear slices on top.

2 To make the cake, cream the butter and sugar in a bowl until light and fluffy. Gradually beat in the eggs and flour until smooth, then mix in the orange rind and juice.

3 Spoon the cake mixture over the pears, level the surface and bake in a preheated oven, 180°C (350°F), Gas Mark 4, for 1–1¼ hours until well risen and golden and a skewer inserted into the centre comes out clean. Check after 45 minutes and cover with foil if the cake appears to be browning too quickly.

4 Loosen the edges of the cake, cover it with a large plate, then invert the tin on to the plate and remove. Spoon a little cranberry sauce over the top while still hot. Serve warm or cold, cut into wedges with whipped cream and a dusting of sifted icing sugar.

TIP
Frozen cranberries can be used instead of fresh, but be sure to defrost them thoroughly first.

Toffee apple muffin

This makes a great standby and you will find that few people can resist it. During cooking, the sugar melts to form a deliciously smooth, toffee-like sauce for the apples. It is perfect served with homemade vanilla ice cream.

1 Toss the apples in a shallow, ovenproof dish with 1 tablespoonful of the flour and the muscovado sugar.

2 Mix the remaining flour with the caster sugar and mixed spice in a bowl. Add the egg, yogurt and butter and stir lightly until only just combined.

3 Spoon the mixture over the apples and bake in a preheated oven, 220°C (425°F), Gas Mark 7, for 15–20 minutes until they are just firm and golden. Serve warm.

3 **dessert apples**, cored and thickly sliced

100 g (3½ oz) **self-raising flour**, plus 1 tablespoon extra

125 g (4 oz) **light muscovado sugar**

50 g (2 oz) **caster sugar**

½ teaspoon **ground mixed spice**

1 **egg**

100 ml (3½ fl oz) **natural yogurt**

50 g (2 oz) **unsalted butter**, melted

Serves 4
*Preparation time: **10 minutes***
*Cooking time: **15–20 minutes***

1 tablespoon **cocoa powder**

1 tablespoon **boiling water**

125 g (4 oz) soft **margarine**
or **butter**, at room
temperature

2 **eggs**

125 g (4 oz) **caster sugar**

125 g (4 oz) **self-raising flour**

To decorate:

150 g (5 oz) **plain dark
chocolate**, broken into pieces

1 tablespoon **cocoa powder**

1 tablespoon **boiling water**

50 g (2 oz) **butter**, at room
temperature

125 g (4 oz) **icing sugar**

6 **glacé cherries**

1 small packet of **candy-
coated chocolate sweets**

Makes 12
Preparation time: **40 minutes**
Cooking time: **13–15 minutes**

Reindeer cupcakes

These fun-sized chocolate cupcakes will bring a festive smile to the face of any small child. They are decorated with chocolates and candied cherries for an authentic Rudolph nose.

1 Line a 12-section bun tin with paper cake cases. Put the cocoa powder into a bowl and mix to a smooth paste with the boiling water.

2 Put all the remaining cake ingredients into a bowl and beat until smooth. Stir in the cocoa paste then divide the mixture between the paper cake cases. Bake the cupcakes in a preheated oven, 180°C (350°F), Gas Mark 4, for 13–15 minutes until they are well risen and spring back when pressed with a fingertip. Leave to cool.

3 Meanwhile, place the chocolate in a heatproof bowl and melt over a saucepan of gently simmering water. Spoon melted chocolate into a greaseproof paper piping bag, snip off the tip, and pipe lines of chocolate about 6 cm

(2½ inches) long on a baking tray lined with nonstick baking paper. Pipe on small branches for antlers. Make enough for two per cake with extras in case of breakages. Leave to dry and harden.

4 Mix the cocoa powder with the boiling water in a large bowl. Add the butter then gradually beat in the icing sugar to make a smooth icing. Spread the icing over the tops of the cupcakes. Add a halved cherry for a nose and 2 little sweets for eyes, piping on the remaining melted chocolate to make eyeballs. Peel the antlers off the parchment paper and stick at angles into the cupcakes. Store the cupcakes in a cool place until ready to serve.

125 g (4 oz) **butter**

125 ml (4 fl oz) **maple syrup**

125 g (4 oz) **light muscovado sugar**

225 g (7½ oz) **self-raising flour**

1 teaspoon **baking powder**

1 teaspoon **ground ginger**

2 **eggs**

125 ml (4 fl oz) **milk**

3 tablespoons **glacé ginger**, chopped, plus extra to decorate

Icing:

200 g (7 oz) **icing sugar**, sifted

4 teaspoons **water**

2 pieces **glacé ginger**, sliced

Makes 12
*Preparation time: **30 minutes**, plus setting*
*Cooking time: **10–15 minutes***

Snow-covered ginger muffins

Light, moist and very tasty, these icing-crowned muffins taste delicious with cups of steaming cappuccino or hot chocolate.

1 Line 12 sections of a deep bun tin with paper cake cases. Put the butter, syrup and sugar into a saucepan and heat gently, stirring until the butter has melted. Mix the flour, baking powder and ground ginger in a bowl. Beat the eggs and milk in another bowl.

2 Take the butter pan off the heat, then beat in the flour mixture. Gradually beat in the egg and milk mixture, then stir in the glacé ginger. Divide the mixture evenly among the cake cases and bake in a preheated oven, 180°C (350°F), Gas Mark 4, for 10–15 minutes until well risen and cracked. Leave to cool.

3 Sift the icing sugar into a bowl and gradually mix in the water to create a smooth spoonable icing. Drizzle random lines of icing from a spoon over the muffins and complete with slices of ginger. Leave to harden for 30 minutes before serving.

200 g (7 oz) **white chocolate**, broken into pieces

125 g (4 oz) **butter**

3 **eggs**

175 g (6 oz) **caster sugar**

1 teaspoon **vanilla extract**

150 g (5 oz) **plain flour**

1 teaspoon **baking powder**

75 g (3 oz) **dried cranberries**

Makes 20
*Preparation time: **25 minutes***
*Cooking time: **20–25 minutes***

Cranberry blondies

These moist white-chocolate brownies, packed with chunky pieces of white chocolate and ruby-red cranberries, are a terrific seasonal treat.

1 Line an 18 x 28 x 5 cm (7 x 11 x 2 inch) roasting tin with a large piece of nonstick baking paper and snip diagonally into the corners so that the paper fits snugly over the base and up the sides of the tin.

2 Place half of the chocolate and the butter in a heatproof bowl and melt over a saucepan of gently simmering water. Whisk the eggs, sugar and vanilla in a separate bowl with an electric whisk until light and frothy and the whisk leaves a trail when lifted above the mixture.

3 Fold the melted chocolate and butter mixture into the beaten eggs with a large metal spoon. Sift the flour and baking powder over the top and then fold in gently. Chop the remaining chocolate and fold half of it into the mixture with half the cranberries.

4 Pour the mixture into the lined tin and sprinkle with the rest of the diced chocolate and cranberries. Bake in a preheated oven, 180°C (350°F), Gas Mark 4, for 30–35 minutes until well risen; the top of the cake should be crusty and golden and the centre still slightly soft. Leave to cool in the tin. Lift the paper and cake out of the tin, peel off the paper and cut into squares to serve.

TIP
Many roasting tins have sloping sides, so measure the base dimensions when choosing one.

125 g (4 oz) **butter**

125 g (4 oz) **muscovado sugar**

125 ml (4 fl oz) **double cream**

3 **eggs**

75 g (3 oz) **caster sugar**

150 g (5 oz) **plain flour**

1 teaspoon **baking powder**

Icing:

50 g (2 oz) **butter**

65 g (2½ oz) **light muscovado sugar**

4 tablespoons **double cream**

75 g (3 oz) **plain dark chocolate**, broken into pieces

Makes 15

*Preparation time: **25 minutes**, plus cooling*

*Cooking time: **25–30 minutes***

Butterscotch brownies

Everyone will be clamouring for seconds with these wonderfully light, toffee brownies.

1 Line an 18 x 28 x 5 cm (7 x 11 x 2 inch) roasting tin with a large piece of nonstick baking paper and snip diagonally into the corners so that the paper fits snugly over the base and up the sides of the tin.

2 Put the butter and sugar into a small saucepan and heat gently until the butter has melted and the sugar has dissolved. Take off the heat and stir in the cream. Whisk the eggs and caster sugar in a bowl until light and frothy and the whisk leaves a trail when lifted out of the mixture.

3 Fold the butterscotch mixture into the eggs with a metal spoon. Sift over the flour and baking powder then fold in. Pour into the lined tin. Bake in a preheated oven, 180°C (350°F), Gas Mark 4, for 25–30 minutes until well risen; the top should be crusty and the centre just set. Leave to cool for 15 minutes.

4 Lift the brownies out of the pan by holding the paper lining, place on a wire rack and peel the paper away from the sides. To make the icing, heat the butter and sugar in a saucepan until the sugar has dissolved and the butter has melted. Add the cream and stir over medium heat for 2 minutes. Pour over the brownies and spread in an even layer – don't worry if a little drizzles down the sides. Leave to cool for 15 minutes.

5 Place the chocolate in a heatproof bowl and melt over a saucepan of gently simmering water. Drizzle random squiggles over the butterscotch frosting then leave the brownies to cool completely. Cut into squares and peel off the baking paper.

Cranberry, oatmeal and cinnamon scones

These sweet, cranberry-speckled scones are best served freshly baked. Alternatively, make them in advance, freeze and warm through before serving.

1 Grease a baking sheet. Place the flour, baking powder and cinnamon in a food processor. Add the butter and process until the mixture resembles breadcrumbs. Add the sugar and oatmeal and blend briefly. Alternatively, use your fingertips to rub the butter into the flour, baking powder and cinnamon in a bowl, then add the sugar and oatmeal.

2 Add the cranberries and milk and blend briefly until the mixture forms a soft dough, adding a little more milk if necessary. Turn out on to a floured surface and roll out to a 1.5 cm (¾ inch) thickness. Cut out rounds using a 5 cm (2 inch) cutter. Transfer to the prepared baking sheet and reroll the trimmings to make more scones.

3 Brush the scones with beaten egg or milk and sprinkle with oatmeal. Bake in a preheated oven, 220°C (425°F), Gas Mark 7, for 10–12 minutes until risen and golden, then transfer to a wire rack to cool. Serve split and buttered.

175 g (6 oz) **self-raising flour**

1 teaspoon **baking powder**

1 teaspoon **ground cinnamon**

75 g (3 oz) unsalted **butter**, cut into small pieces

75 g (3 oz) **caster sugar**

50 g (2 oz) **oatmeal**, plus extra for sprinkling

75 g (3 oz) **dried cranberries**

5–6 tablespoons **milk**

beaten **egg** or **milk**, to glaze

Makes 10
*Preparation time: **10 minutes***
*Cooking time: **10–12 minutes***

250 g (8 oz) **puff pastry**, thawed if frozen

flour, for dusting

1 **egg yolk**

2 tablespoons **milk**

18 squares of **plain dark chocolate**

1 teaspoon grated **orange rind**

1 pinch of **ground star anise**

butter, for greasing

Makes 9
*Preparation time: **15 minutes***
*Cooking time: **12 minutes***

Spiced chocolate pastries

Oozing with molten chocolate, these unusual pastries are delicious with tea or freshly brewed coffee.

1 Grease a baking sheet. Roll out the pastry thinly on a lightly floured surface and trim to form a 23 cm (9 inch) square. Cut into thirds crossways and lengthwise to form 9 squares.

2 Beat the egg yolk and milk to make a glaze and brush a little around the edges of each pastry square. Place 2 squares of chocolate, a little orange rind and a touch of star anise on each one. Fold diagonally in half and press the edges together to seal.

3 Place the pastries on the prepared baking sheet and bake in a preheated oven, 200°C (400°F), Gas Mark 6, for 12 minutes, until risen and golden. Leave them to cool on a wire rack for a few minutes before serving.

Layered nutty bars

These no-bake chocolate refrigerator bars can be mixed quickly and then left to chill. Serve as part of afternoon tea or cut into tiny bite-sized pieces to make petits fours.

1 Use a little of the butter to grease the base and sides of a 20 cm (8 inch) round springform tin. Put the rest of the butter into a saucepan with the condensed milk and chocolate. Heat gently for 3–4 minutes, stirring until melted, then remove from the heat.

2 Put the biscuits into a plastic bag and roughly crush into chunky pieces with a rolling pin. Toast the hazelnuts under a preheated hot grill until lightly browned, then roughly chop with the pistachios.

3 Stir the biscuits into the chocolate mixture then spoon half the mixture into the prepared tin and spread flat. Reserve 2 tablespoons of the nuts for the top, then sprinkle the rest over the chocolate biscuit layer. Cover with the remaining chocolate

mixture, level the top with the back of the spoon and sprinkle with the reserved nuts.

4 Chill the nut mixture for 3–4 hours until firm, then loosen the edge of the tin and remove the sides. Cut into thin slices. Any leftovers can be stored in the refrigerator, wrapped in foil, for up to 3 days.

TIP
Glacé cherries or ginger, sultanas or dried apricots can be added instead of some of the nuts.

50 g (2 oz) **butter**

400 g (13 oz) **fat-free sweetened condensed milk**

200 g (7 oz) **plain dark chocolate**, broken into pieces

125 g (4 oz) **rich tea biscuits**

50 g (2 oz) **hazelnuts**

100 g (3½ oz) **pistachio nuts**

Serves 10
*Preparation time: **20 minutes**, plus chilling*
*Cooking time: **3–4 minutes***

50 g (2 oz) **blanched hazelnuts**

125 g (4 oz) **butter**, softened, plus extra for greasing

50 g (2 oz) **caster sugar**

150 g (5 oz) **plain flour**

Makes 20
Preparation time: **10 minutes**
Cooking time: **12 minutes**

Quick hazelnut melts

These hazelnut cookies literally melt in your mouth.

1 Grease a baking sheet. Grind the hazelnuts in a food processor or blender until fairly smooth but still retaining a little texture. Brown in a heavy-based frying pan over a low heat until evenly golden. Pour into a bowl and stir until cool.

2 Blend the butter and sugar in a food processor until creamy. Add the flour and cooled nuts and blend again to make a soft dough.

3 Take walnut-sized pieces of dough and shape into balls, then pat into flat ovals. Place on the greased baking sheet and flatten slightly with a fork. Bake in a preheated oven, 190°C (375°F), Gas Mark 5, for 12 minutes, until just golden. Cool on a wire rack. These little cakes can be stored in an airtight container for up to 3 days.

2 teaspoons **cocoa powder**, plus extra to decorate

25 ml (1 fl oz) **Kahlua coffee liqueur**

100 ml (3½ fl oz) **filter coffee**

mini marshmallows

whipped cream

Serves 1
*Preparation time: **5 minutes***
*Cooking time: **3 minutes***

Marshmallow mocha

An indulgent, chocolaty version of Irish coffee, with melted marshmallows and whipped cream on top. This makes a great follow-up to a light dessert at a dinner party.

1 Put the cocoa powder in a toddy glass, add the Kahlua and coffee and stir until mixed. Drop in the mini marshmallows and float the cream on top. Decorate with a sprinkling of cocoa powder.

Festive hot chocolate

Thick and luscious hot chocolate topped with a frothy white cloud of cream and melting marshmallows is wonderfully indulgent and heart-warming. If you really want to spoil yourself, add a few tablespoons of brandy.

1 Pour the milk into a saucepan and bring just to the boil. Remove the pan from heat and add the chocolate, sugar, cinnamon and marshmallows. Leave to stand for 2–3 minutes.

2 Meanwhile, whip the cream in a bowl until it is just beginning to thicken and form soft peaks. Using a whisk, beat the milk mixture in the saucepan until frothy. Pour into cups or mugs and spoon the cream on top.

3 Decorate each cup or mug with a few extra marshmallows and a sprinkling of cinnamon. Serve immediately.

750 ml (1¼ pints) **full cream milk**

100 g (3½ oz) **plain dark chocolate**, broken into pieces

50 g (2 oz) **caster sugar**

a little **ground cinnamon**

125 g (4 oz) **marshmallows**, plus extra to serve

125 ml (4 fl oz) **double cream**

Makes 4 cups or 2 large mugs
*Preparation time: **5 minutes***
*Cooking time: **3 minutes***

crushed **ice**

1.8 litres (3 pints) **cranberry juice**

600 ml (1 pint) **orange juice**

600 ml (1 pint) **ginger ale**

cocktail cherries, lemon slices and **lime spirals,** to decorate

Serves 15

*Preparation time: **5 minutes***

Cranberry crush

A tempting fruit punch with a seasonal theme, perfect for Christmas parties with all age groups.

1 Half-fill a punch bowl with crushed ice. Pour in the cranberry and orange juices and stir to mix. Fill to the brim with the ginger ale and decorate with cocktail cherries, lemon slices and lime spirals. Serve immediately.

TIP
For a special party, float red rose petals on the top of the punch.

90 ml (3 fl oz) **grenadine**

90 ml (3 fl oz) **vodka**

seeds from 1 **pomegranate**

1 **lime,** thinly sliced (optional)

1 bottle **sparkling dry white wine,** well chilled

Serves 6

*Preparation time: **5 minutes***

Pomegranate punch

This vibrant pink punch looks innocent enough but it has a hidden kick, so warn drivers and children to steer clear.

1 Divide the grenadine and vodka between 6 champagne flutes, then add the pomegranate seeds and lime slices, if using. Top up with the sparkling wine and serve at once.

TIPS
To remove the pomegranate seeds, cut the pomegranate in half, then break it into pieces and pop out the pink seeds. For a less alcoholic punch, half-fill the glasses with cranberry and apple juice, then add the vodka and a little less wine.

1 litre (1¾ pints) **orange juice**

2 litres (3½ pints) **red grape juice**

juice of 6 **lemons**

juice of 6 **limes**

sugar syrup, to taste

20–30 **ice cubes**

orange, **lemon** and **lime** slices, to decorate

Serves 15
Preparation time: 5 minutes

Holiday sangria

Sangria puts everyone into a holiday mood. This non-alcoholic version is thirst-quenching and delicious.

1 Pour the orange juice into a punch bowl. Add the grape, lemon and lime juices and stir to mix. Add sugar syrup to taste and stir well. Add the ice, then float the fruit slices on top.

TIP
To make sugar syrup, boil equal quantities of sugar and water until the sugar has dissolved then allow to cool.

FOR ALCOHOLIC SANGRIA
Substitute red wine for the grape juice and add 175 ml (6 fl oz) of brandy.

2 tablespoons **brandy**

2 tablespoons **dark rum**

1 **egg**

1 teaspoon **sugar syrup**

75 ml (3 fl oz) **full-cream milk**

grated **nutmeg**, to decorate

Serves 1
Preparation time: 5 minutes

Egg nog

This traditional winter drink served dusted with grated nutmeg will bring out the Christmas spirit in anyone. Serve to special guests.

1 Put the brandy, rum, egg and sugar syrup into a cocktail shaker and shake well, then strain into a large goblet. Add the milk, stir gently, then decorate with a little grated nutmeg.

Index

Food stylist: Sara Lewis
Special Photography: Lis Parsons/
© Octopus Publishing Group Ltd